33 LETTERS OF COMPASSION

33 LETTERS OF COMPASSION

To: The Unseen
Love, Rosie

Written by: Elaine Elizabeth

Edited by: Mike Wood

Copyright © 2023 Elaine Elizabeth

All rights reserved No part of this book may be reproduced or used in any way without the prior permission of the copyright owner, except for brief quotes in literary work

To request permissions, contact the publisher at
elaine@generationalevolution.life

Hardcover ISBN: 979-8-88759-637-2
Paperback ISBN: 979-8-88759-585-6
Ebook ISBN: 979-8-88759-586-3
Audiobook ISBN: 979-8-88759-638-9

First Paperback 2023
Edited by Mike Wood
Cover Design by Elaine Elizabeth

Contents

I:	To The Unseen, ...9
II:	To My Suicidal Thoughts, ...11
III:	To PTSD Triggers Everywhere, ...14
IV:	To The Human Who Fights Their Own Battles, ...17
V:	To The One That Has Been Hurt So Many Times, ...19
VI:	Dear Lost One, ...22
VII:	To The Piece of Me I'm Afraid to Expose, ...24
VIII:	To The Thing Inside That Demands Perfection, ...26
IX:	Dear Control Room, ...28
X:	To The Angry Gremlin Staying Inside My House, ...31
XI:	To My Depression, ...33
XII:	Dear Human, ...35
XIII:	To The Childhood I Barely Remember, ...37
XIV:	To The Abused One, ...40
XV:	To The Hurt Child, ...43
XVI:	To The Kid Who Works The System, ...45
XVII:	To The Child Staring Back at Me, ...47
XVIII:	To The Foreman in My Brain, ...49

XIX:	To The Elusive Concept of Love,	51
XX:	To The Daughter Who Grew Up with a Narcissistic Mother,	53
XXI:	To My Authentic Self,	55
XXII:	To My Soul,	57
XXIII:	To The Glass Ceiling,	59
XXIV:	To The Piece of Happiness Inside,	61
XXV:	To The One Who Chose To Stay,	63
XXVI:	Dear Time,	65
XXVII:	To My Invisible Mirror,	67
XXVIII:	To The One Who Is Too Much to Handle,	70
XXIX:	To The Abandoned One,	72
XXX:	To My Anxiety,	75
XXXI:	To My Inner Strength,	76
XXXII:	To The Unhealed Version of Me,	78
XXXIII:	To The Unseen,	80
References		83

I

To The Unseen,

Here you are. Reading a letter from the author. Weird. However, I think it's required to have a foreword; this is my version.

The letters you're about to read are sometimes heavy, but hopefully empowering. You can read them in order or out of order. You will discover something in whatever way you read it. I hope you find this book at the right time in your life. Just know what I wrote down wasn't for you originally. I wrote these letters for pieces of myself or recipients I needed to have compassion for. The 33 letters started out as a healthy ritual I adapted from an old friend to practice compassion.

Before this book was published, I read one letter to a meditation group. The letter was "To The One That Has Been Hurt So Many Times". After reading it, they asked if I would read another letter the next week. It snowballed into a collection of letters and a habit of reading one letter each week. Every Friday I connect to their energy and read a letter. Each letter stirs something different in each person. But each listener feels heard in some way. I'm hoping you do, too.

With Love, Rosie

II

To My Suicidal Thoughts,

You're extremely loud sometimes...

Sometimes it takes every fiber of my being just to keep you at bay.

Yes, I'm well aware that I have a choice to stay on this rock we call Earth or to leave. That is completely my choice. Right now, there is nothing keeping me here. If I stay I have to fight to stay alive.

It gets beyond exhausting treading water. I feel like I am going to sink at any moment and no one will hear me. Drowning is actually a silent act. No one knows until you can't find the person.

Suicidal Thoughts, you're something I was not trained for. School never taught me how to handle what I went through. No one gave me tools for this. Everyone keeps trying to convince me to stay because they love me.

The hardest part about that is that it bounces off like water on a duck's back. It means nothing to me.

I can't connect to "I love you" because that is NOT what is happening inside my head. I don't feel good enough to be here. I don't feel like I have the strength it will take to get me out of this hole.

It's daunting looking up and seeing how far I've sunk. I want to be a part of the surface world but I feel like I am too far under the water. The pressure is caving in and it's hard to breathe. Every breath that I take reminds me that I am still alive when all I want is to not be here.

But maybe that's my issue. I've trained my brain to focus on the past and the negative so I forget about the small perfect moments. They are painful to watch because I wish it was me, but you know the moments. A baby giggling at a silly face. A friend's hug at the right time. A perfect meal that a family member used to make.

Buddha talks about watering the good seeds versus the bad seeds. I wonder if that is what he is talking about. Turning my focus on the good versus the bad. It sounds so simple. It's still daunting and I don't want to do it, but maybe he's right. I am in control of where I put my energy. I've been so focused on what happened that I can't see the good right in front of me.

I can't promise anything, Suicidal Thoughts. But maybe over time, I can have more positive thoughts instead of all the negative. I'm still so tired of treading water. Maybe I need to start swimming to shore instead.

Best Regards, Your Human

III

To PTSD Triggers Everywhere,

I fucking loathe you.

Yeah. I said it. I hate you. You absolute pieces of shit. Every goddamn one of you knows what you do. You triggers pop up at the most inconvenient times and each of you beyond disrupts my day.

I can't describe to you the amount of frustration I have when you pop up. I have no control over it. Most days I don't even know how or why you're a trigger. It's like you're trying to loudly get my attention and I don't want anything to do with you! Why would I? You're everything that happened ALL AT ONCE!!!

You're a straight bullet to the heart. You flood my brain with negative hormones that trigger the fight or flight response. You fuck everything up and I don't even know why!!

It's like you're trying to communicate with me but you speak another language that is painful to me. What do you want from me?! Haven't I suffered enough?!?

What do you want me to do, look back at the trauma and recognize I had no control??

What happened is exactly what happened.

Next you'll say that I have to put in work to heal rather than run away from it. Yeah, right! Like that's ever going to happen. You are fucking painful. Why would I want to turn and face the trauma? That's fucking insane.

That would mean that I would have to take responsibility for my own pain. I couldn't blame anyone else... no one is inflicting pain on me now... I'm just reliving the past...because of me...I'm giving myself pain.

Fuck.

But that's not right. You're painful to me! How can you mean something else?

It's like my brain lied to me about what you are.

Fuck.

I can understand why.

My brain went into protective mode. It saw you as a threat because last time it was a real one. So my brain created a defense mechanism. Logical. Protect at all costs.

But seriously? Why this way? Why use something so painful to try to communicate?!

Probably because I wouldn't pay attention otherwise. I've been pretending to be okay. Motherfucker. You had to be loud so I'd pay attention? Well, I'm listening now. What do you fucking want?

Goddammit! Each one of you triggers is like a new lesson or test as it were to see if my mindset is manifesting outwardly. You pieces of shit.

If that's how you're going to play, every trigger that comes my way, I'll process and learn so I'm smarter for the next one. Getting more keen until you don't phase me anymore. For fuck sake. If it's a fight you want, a fight you'll get.

I'll retrain my brain to take responsibility for my day. The past can't hurt me if I learn to stay in the present moment. If I let the past control my actions today I stay in the same place like a puppet on a string. I don't want to be a fucking puppet anymore.

Your Young Military Widow with a Sailor's Mouth

IV

To The Human Who Fights Their Own Battles,

I call bullshit. You heard me. I call bullshit. How can you fight your own battles when you haven't even learned to love the should-be winning team? How strong is your army? How much time do you spend with the troops? Do you feed them? Do you give them weapons?

If you're trying to fight your own battles, your base should be strong. Your mental health should be strong. And yet saying "these are my demons to fight" is not allowing support. Yes, no one can fight the demons for you. But support can give you food to feed your army. Tools you learn from other people allow you to fight your own demons.

You're right. Those are your fights. But what if you had weapons from different countries? Different advice and knowledge to fight against the demons inside your head?

Don't be too quick to deny help. They aren't there to fight your battles. They are there to support. So good luck fighting your own battles. You can either just use *your* supply of guns and ammo or you can have access to so many more weapons. It's up to you.

Love, Your Human

V

To The One That Has Been Hurt So Many Times,

I see you. I see the way that you act. You have your heart surrounded by walls. You lash out at anyone who gets close to the protective castle. You live in fear that trusting them with the thing inside will only hurt your heart more. Why risk it? If you treat people outside the wall like shit, they will leave. The threat of hurt will leave.

In reality your subconscious is being protective the only way it knows how. Spread the pain to avoid the pain. Thinking it can get rid of it. "They can't hurt me if I hurt them first."

You have to look inside the castle of your own heart to mend it. How can you mend something you don't even acknowledge or spend time with?

You just protect.

Your soul wants time with you. But no one can do it for you. You're waiting for someone to save you but your castle is too strong. You're the only person. The strongest person to break down those walls because you're the only one who can do it with love.

Reality is, You don't trust anyone else to take care of your heart. You haven't even figured out how to take care of it yourself. So how can they know how to?

So, to the one on the floor crying because of life, recognize you have to be your own savior. You can lash out all you want, but that's not going to heal you. I'm sorry that you're hurting. It's shitty, I know.

But look at the whole picture before you think someone is out to get you. No one is. The way people interact with other people is how they treat themselves. So if you're lashing out, that just tells me you're in pain and you need healthy love. To show you that you're seen. So who cares if this letter is sappy or too positive. You have a choice if it hurts you. Most people aren't trying to hurt. They hurt others because they haven't healed those pieces yet. They don't know what they are doing.

After this letter, you know. You understand that you are in charge of how you interact with other people. It's not easy having this knowledge. And you'll slip up, but that's okay. At least you're working on healing.

One last note, If you spend time nurturing me at the end of each day. You can focus on healing the day's emotions and triggers. Keep doing that, and over time there won't be trapped emotions. It's a daily energetic cleanse.

With Love, Your Soul

VI

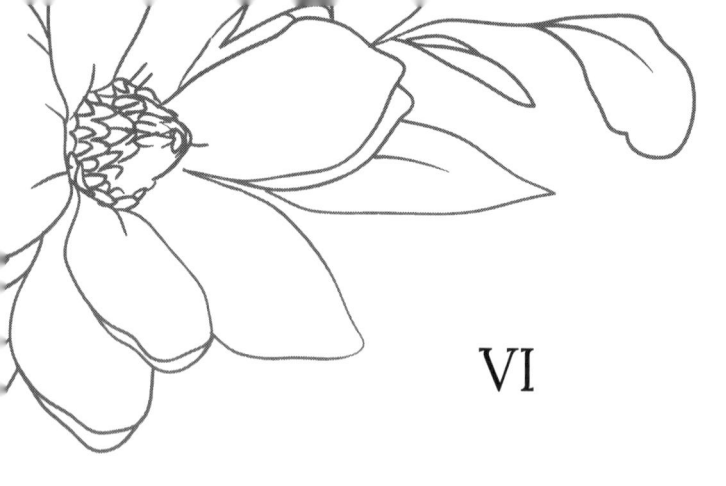

Dear Lost One,

It's okay to feel lost. It really is. When you feel lost it's a good place to start building. I know that sounds too positive, but think about it.

If you didn't feel lost, it means you've been there before. But I'm not sure if you want to be back there anymore. It didn't seem like you liked it. Being lost doesn't have to be scary. Yes, in the beginning it is, but then you start looking around at all the new scenery.

Essentially, think of the pioneers. They had no clue where they were going. They may have had some sort of map, but not like what we have now. They recognized that if they wanted a better life, they'd move forward. They wouldn't stay where they were.

Our society has lied to you. Change isn't bad. Change provides an opportunity to learn new things. If nothing ever changed, we'd still be single cell organisms right now.

You can either see change as a hurdle to get over or you can see change as an opportunity to learn new skills.

Yeah, it might suck right now and you feel like there is no direction. Here's a little secret: it's the perfect time for you to choose a direction. It's completely up to you how you choose to get unlost. It will take work and dedication and you are worth it. You got this!

You are in control of your life. You may feel lost because you have never felt like you had the opportunity to take control over your life. Maybe now is that time to take control. Just something that helped me get unlost.

Love, Someone Who Once Felt Lost

VII

To The Piece of Me I'm Afraid to Expose,

I've put you in a bubble that no one else can touch, in fear that someone won't accept you.

I've been lying.

You're in a bubble because I'm afraid to accept you.

I myself struggle with seeing you with love. I'm embarrassed of you. I want to deal with you before anyone else gets their hands on you, but I'm realizing I have to supply the strength. No one else can give me the strength to love you.

It's difficult because society says I should be ashamed. That I should find someone else to love that piece of me first.

Why? Why should I be ashamed of you? Society says because I'm in the wrong. If I flip my mindset, I could say I'm not in the wrong. It was a learning point. A piece of myself that teaches me.

So, piece of me that I don't want to expose, what do you have to teach me?

I'll take a deep breath and accept that it's okay. It's okay to learn from you. You're there to remind me of something or to show me an opportunity to grow.

I see you with compassion.

It's difficult, but I love you. You don't have to live in a bubble anymore. I accept you for what you are. You are a Lego in my build.

I appreciate you. You are a new piece to work with to become my authentic self. I don't have to expose you to the world, I have to expose you to myself. I have to pop the bubble in order to accept you. To learn from you. I look forward to finding out what you have to teach me.

With Love, Your Human

VIII

To The Thing Inside That Demands Perfection,

I'm sorry.

I'm sorry that your stomach won't ever get filled. It's impossible. It must be so frustrating at times to feel starved. I can't imagine how maddening it is. To want something and never get it.

The hunger you feel is made up. It's something you have convinced yourself you need. If you demand perfection, that just shows me you haven't learned how to accept that societal expectations are made up. Literally.

Every culture has its own expectations. It just depends what culture you grew up in. Cultural expectations are things we are born around but get to choose to accept or reject. That's the thing.

Take a step back and realize you have so much free will. A so-called "mistake" is so misunderstood. So much so, you're missing out on growth! Society calls it a mistake. I'm going to tell you a secret. It's actually the universe providing an opportunity to learn.

You fuck up, okay. It's up to you how you're going to face it. You could use it as a weapon on yourself. Beating yourself up over and over again about one action. That's up to you. Or you can use it as a Lego in your Lego build. Life isn't a map. You're not going anywhere. In fact, you're building wherever you go. Every "mistake", every interaction with someone is a new Lego for your build.

So to the thing that demands perfection, start demanding Legos. Start building instead of doing damage. Please. I implore you to look at the Legos in your life and make something beautiful. You won't be disappointed.

I hope to hear from you soon. I know this is a lot to take in and process. Hearing that perfection isn't the goal but rather creating can be a brain twister. So don't forget to take a breath and remember mistakes aren't bad as long as you learn from them and use them in your Lego build.

Until Next Time, Your Human

IX

Dear Control Room,

I started this letter to ask questions. But then I stopped myself because maybe you don't know the answers either. Maybe you're there to manage but no one is there to train you. It's not like there is another control tower in there that you can talk to. You're trying to manage a lot. You have a lot on your plate. You have to manage food intake, hormone intake, hormone output, waste output. And that's just the physical side of things. That doesn't even include relationships with family and friends. Societal expectations. Your own expectations. You're the control room, no wonder you feel like you're spinning. There is a lot to control.

There is so much you have to deal with and it seems like there is no manual. That's the funny part. It's still being written and edited to manage each season of this life. The manual is ever evolving and you're the writer. You get to write the manual on how to manage the control room. The catch is, you can only write the manual for you. Everyone else has to write their own manual. Control room, you get to control how this version of this life goes. You get to decide how to handle all of the things either in a healthy way or an unhealthy way.

Control room, there is Internet in there. I hooked it up when you were becoming an adult. That means you can research how to manage this thing called life. You have the power to research and test out what works for you if you really want to take back control of the control room. Authors like Eckhart Tolle, Chris Bailey, Thich Nhat Hanh, Daniel Quinn and so many other writers have provided opportunities to grow. You don't have to stare at the flashing red lights and the sirens going off in your head. There is a way for the control room to run smoothly. Take one thing at a time and spend time getting to know the controls.

How often do you avoid your own thoughts because they are negative? Avoid by exercising, playing video games or music, wasting time on social media or so many other distractions. Why can't you see that the only way to make it peaceful in there is if you make it peaceful. You have to do the work to make your control room beautiful which means being nice to it. It's wild how people think that they don't have a choice of what they hear inside their control room. They think they are the loudspeakers in the office talking shit. The truth is, they are the controller standing there listening.

The control room can switch to a different station. A station that promotes peace. The new station talks about how to be kind to the person who's in control, not how to destroy the control room. As a reminder, you are not running the show, control room, the controller is. Let the controller teach you how to run smoothly.

With Love, Your Soul

X

To The Angry Gremlin Staying Inside My House,

What's going on?! How can I help you?! I watch you thrash around, throwing plates and bowls, screaming at the ceiling. I stand in awe not knowing how to help.

It's like you're out of control and you yourself can't get a foothold on reality. Your head is spinning, seeing red, wanting to burn my house down!

What do you need in this moment to feel safe? What would help you take a breath and sit with me to communicate what's going on. I'm here to help you. Not to hurt you. I wish I could grab you and squeeze you until all the rage is gone. I want to grab your face and, with a loving tone, say, "Hey! It's going to be okay! You're not alone. I see you. I see the pain. I see the wounds and all I want to do is do everything in my power to help! I don't like seeing you like this."

Gremlin, do you even know why you're mad?

It must be confusing sometimes to have these emotions and not understand them. I could suggest every tool in the book to "calm" you down but honestly, the biggest thing I can do for you is to say:

> *"It's okay. It's okay to be mad sometimes. Don't try to change that emotion. Just accept that you're mad and that it's okay to be mad. The only catch is: Watch how you use your anger."*

Gremlin, I wish I could physically be there for you but all I can do is write a letter to tell you that you don't have to destroy my house to get attention.

Gremlin, you visit my house and that's okay. When you come, I'm going to do my best to remind you that it's okay to feel, just don't forget to figure out why and what would help you see the situation out of love. Love for yourself and for whoever or whatever brought you to my house. Gremlin, you show me what I need to work on and, for that, thank you. I may not like you at times but I'm grateful that you visit to show me the green flags to go and heal myself or to work on communication or boundaries. Whatever I need to work on, I will. I am in charge of my own happiness.

With Love, Your Human

XI

To My Depression,

I feel like a lot of people have written letters to their depression. I may just be one of a thousand. But, I'd like to talk to you.

I know you're not me. I know this because you don't make me feel like myself. You make it difficult to get up in the morning. You make it difficult to do the dishes, to take a shower, to do laundry, to brush my teeth!!! You make my daily life difficult!!

I want to expel you from my apartment and yet you stay!! Buddha says everyone is a mirror. So if I want you to go, what part of me do I see in you that I don't like? What do I need to accept and change?

I know you're an abstract concept, but if I talk to you as if you're a person I can separate myself from you. You are not my identity. I know you're not because I don't want to be you! I want to be me, but you make it so difficult!!!

Depression, you may be here as a red flag to tell me I need to change my habits, but from what I know about behaviors, it will take time. I won't see the results right away. Society has lied to me and made it seem like I should see immediate results.

It's laughable because that's not how evolution works! That's what I'm trying to do. I'm trying to evolve. I'm trying to maintain healthy habits and yet you're here! Making it difficult!!

I know I'm worth getting back to feeling like myself. I am worth changing my habits to retrain my brain to create an unfit environment for you so you can leave. I know substance is your guilty pleasure. Mainly because it makes me numb and that's what depression is. I want to escape from the problems at hand.

What I also know is that you won't go away until I turn and face you. If I ignore that you're there, you'll just get bigger and I don't want that. The longer I wait, the harder it will be to get rid of you. Not impossible, just harder.

So, depression, for right now you may be in my apartment but I'm going to work hard, one habit at a time. Everyone is different and it's okay to work at one thing at a time. Tackling the whole problem is a bit intimidating and I'm not down for that. I'd rather take one bad habit and learn to change it and then go to the next one. Baby steps. That's way more my speed.

With Love, A Future Old Roommate

XII

Dear Human,

It's okay.

It's okay to feel what you're feeling. It's okay to struggle at times. It's okay to feel like you're on cloud nine at weird personal moments. It's okay to feel. They wouldn't be called feelings if they weren't meant to be felt 100%.

Let me try to put it differently. Emotions are encoded notes from your body. An emotion equals a message on how to help the body. For example, anger is usually an encryption for an unmet expectation. Spoken or unspoken.

Ask yourself: "Did I communicate that expectation?" If the answer is yes, you have to decide how you will proceed with the knowledge that they failed to meet an expectation. If the answer is no, meaning you didn't communicate the expectation—The result would hopefully be taking responsibility for not communicating properly and doing better next time.

Emotions are like love letters to the brain, but they're getting lost in translation. The letters aren't supposed to be buried under the bed waiting to be dealt with. They are meant to be opened and dealt with so they don't get piled up. As an adult you can put the envelope in your pocket until you get a moment to yourself to open it.

Childhood is like opening every letter as soon as you get it. Adolescents and young adults do not know when to open their letters because adults haven't figured it out. So there is no blueprint for when to deal with emotions.

I think it isn't until we are much older that we figure out that you can open certain letters later and some letters in the present. I think it depends on the environment. It's truly up to you when you open your letters. But emotions aren't bad. They are just misunderstood. Like a lot of us.

With Love, A Human Who Misread Emotions

XIII

To The Childhood I Barely Remember,

I know you existed. I know that you shaped me into who I am today. Or rather had a season to play to get me to where I am now.

I don't remember you because my brain has categorized you as irrelevant. That was the past. This is the now. But I wonder what the reality of my childhood was like. I only have my lens as a child. But now that I am a parent, I wonder what big picture those who raised me saw that I didn't.

My perception of my childhood is exactly that. A perception. It was only from my point of view. From my parents point of view, they saw the bigger picture.

So what exactly did my childhood look like? I would be lying if I said I never called it toxic at some point. But that was because I didn't see the bigger picture. The bigger picture being those that raised me did their very best with the tools they were given.

They didn't know what they were doing. They still don't know. It's not like they had practice before my sister and I. Maybe some do with multiple children but even then that's chaotic. It's not like someone could practice with a single kid from 0-75 years old and choose to do it again differently in one lifetime.

No wonder kids see their families as toxic. What else are they supposed to do? No one taught them to heal their own trauma before becoming guardians. That's what toxic traits are. Unhealed pieces of ourselves.

We all have toxic traits and that's okay. I guess, childhood, what I wanted to tell you was, thank you. Thank you for showing me that being imperfect is okay. Everyone is doing their best with the tools they have been given. Hopefully trying to learn to be better along the way.

It's okay that I don't really remember you. You did exactly what you were meant to do and I accept it. I accept what happened to me.

I recognize that we all have our own shit to deal with. The only response now is love. Love towards my childhood and those that raised me. Their goal was to raise a healthier generation, and they did. That's why there is a disconnect. They achieved exactly what they set out to do. To make a better life for their child than what they had growing up.

Thank you, childhood. I appreciate your role in my life. I wouldn't be who I am today. I don't forgive those that raised me because that means I'm better than them. I'm not. I'm exactly the same. I do my best every day with the tools I was given. Saying "I forgive you" implies I am right and they are wrong. How can they be wrong when I'm doing the same thing? We are all trying to survive.

Childhood, you've shown me a lot. Thank you.

With Love, Your Human

XIV

To The Abused One,

"I'm sorry."

Two words in the English Language that can never erase what you went through. My hands are tied. No amount of writing can take away the pain. You went through a lot and it has changed you. It has impacted your life in a way that no one can fully understand.

It's an invisible burden that only you know intimately. I can't fix it. No one can.

I genuinely wish I could. I wish I could go back in time and stop what happened to you. I know it changed your entire development. It trapped part of your mind in the past and it's affecting the present.

The people who hurt you were hurt themselves and they didn't know what else to do but try to get rid of it...you were just the closest target. It doesn't excuse what happened.

It's shitty. That's not how it's supposed to be.

Question is, what exactly is "supposed" to happen?

That answer changes every time you ask it.

If you ask a remote tribe somewhere in the middle of nowhere, "What exactly is supposed to happen in childhood?" They may tell you that children are there to run free. No discipline. No specific parents, just a tribe working together as a group to raise children. Adults aren't in monogamous relationships. Because where they are, that's the normal.

Nothing is supposed to happen. Things happen because if they didn't, life would be boring. We have hopes and we have societal expectations of how things are supposed to go but in reality, it's all made up. The societal expectations and structure are all made up.

Yes, I know. It sounds wrong. It's difficult to accept what happened. All I can say is the cliché "Hurt people hurt people". It's just up to you how you walk away from it.

You can either let their pain hurt you, or it can transform you. It can transform the way you see them and how you act after. If you keep seeing them as mean, that is all you will ever see them as. Or, you can see them for who they were when they abused you. They were humans trying to figure it out.

You have to take responsibility for how you treat people now that you're not being abused. You get to choose how you use your abuse.

Sounds weird, but hear me out.

You can continue to use your abuse to react to people in a snappy or untrusting way, or you can use it to have compassion because you know what pain feels like.

You can use your experience to help people NOT feel the pain you experienced. That is a choice. Because deep down you wish those who abused you didn't make you feel like that.

So you have a choice to be better than them. It's up to you.

Best Regards, Someone Who Made The Choice

XV

To The Hurt Child,

I'm deeply inspired by your resilience.

Resilience is a fancy word for recovering from something difficult. I may not know what difficult thing you went through, but I know that you survived.

How do I know? Because you're here reading this letter. You wouldn't be here if you hadn't been resilient.

Yes, what you went through was difficult and terrible. But, look at what it made.

That trauma made *you*.

You magnificent soul.

You have the ability to see pain in others and have empathy because you understand.

That's what empathy is. To understand what someone is going through and have love for them.

Hurt child, what you need to know is that it is up to you on how you use your pain. You could use it to become a victim or you could use it to fight. You could use it to inflict pain on others.

Or, You could use your pain that someone inflicted on you, and transform it. You can stop the cycle.

What if instead of allowing that pain to hurt you, you decide it doesn't need to hurt anymore?

Child who was hurt, you don't have to run from the monsters under your bed anymore. You can turn and face the monsters. They aren't real.

The reality is, you survived and learned a lot from it and I'm sure you've helped people because you went through it.

If you hadn't gone through that difficult thing, you wouldn't have been able to do all of that good.

Thank you. Thank you for staying and being you.

You are so loved and never alone.

With Love, Your Human

XVI

To The Kid Who Works The System,

I see your cleverness. I see your frustration. I see the exhaustion from going back and forth to and from the different houses. You're trying to survive in an unstable environment the only way you know how. By finding loopholes.

To us, it seems like lying and being lazy. When in reality you're smart enough to work the system. You understand that communication is difficult amongst adults so you play on that to get what you want. To find some sort of control in a situation where you feel you have none.

You didn't ask to get shuffled from house to house. I'm sorry. I'm sorry that you feel the need to control the system to feel like you have some control. You get told what to do and different things are being expected at each location.

It must be confusing as all hell not knowing what happened before the shuffling around. You were so young, you had no idea what was going on. So now that you're older, you understand how to work the system.

I wish I could help you. I wish I could help you feel like you don't have to do that anymore. I wish I could explain to you that you're only making your life more difficult by lying and trying to find loopholes. But, I get it. There's no consistency in your life so you're taking the lead and making decisions for yourself for what you think is in your best interest. Because in reality, maybe deep down, you don't think anyone else can do that for you.

Why would you think they would? They have different agendas. Maybe consciously you don't understand that, but subconsciously I think you believe it. How could people who shuffle you around and expect different things have your best interests in mind?

I'm here to tell you they are doing their best. Who knows if they all have your best interests in mind, but I know at least a few of them do. Shuffling you around may be better than staying in a toxic home 24/7.

It's a hard pill to swallow and accept. No one is out to get you. They made decisions to give you a better life. You just may not see it yet and that's okay. You're still very much loved whether you see it or not.

With Love, A Loving Stepmother

XVII

To The Child Staring Back at Me,

I see your innocence. I see your cunning side. I see your mischievous side. I see your hurt ego from your short life. I look at you and it's overwhelming.

You want to know everything and yet you're limited by your developmental speed.

Your speed is 4 miles per hour, but we want you to be in the fast lane with no driver's license.

I'm sorry. I'm so sorry that we don't have a manual. No manual came with you! I wish it did, but every day I'm writing my own manual for my own life in addition to writing a new one for you. A new one including all of the things I've learned from my past to better prepare you for the future. It's a lot.

It's a lot for you and it's a lot for me. I don't know what I'm doing but I'm doing my best to show you unconditional love while trying to teach you about the conditional world ahead.

I wish the world you'll face will be different when you become independent but I can't guarantee that for you. I desperately wish I could but that would be pretending I know everything. I don't. I'm still learning. Just like you.

I hope one day you'll read this with love and know your mom did her best under the circumstances and so did you.

With Love, Your Mom

XVIII

To The Foreman in My Brain,

It has come to my attention that your way of managing the project is insane. You're trying to do the same bad habits from the old job here at the construction site with new guys hoping for better results. As the Site Inspector I am going to have to supersede your authority. I will have to go straight to the Project Manager. I'm going to get him to teach you how to use new ideas and skills to build a more stable structure than last time. It would be great if we had the time to figure things out, but sometimes we just have to buck up. I have to force healthier habits whether I like it or not. I have to match my habits with the season I am in. I'm not motivated to do this. In all honesty, I count to three and just do whatever I need to, to practice healthier habits. Yeah, it's childish, but it helps.

At first there is resistance, and no one said it would be easy. You're trying to change a neurological pathway in your brain. That's like trying to change the course of the Mississippi River in a day. It takes time to establish healthier habits. Just choose one bad habit to work on. Once that one is corrected and a better habit mastered to replace it, pick another bad habit to work on.

So best of luck, Foreman. I'm going to the Project Manager to make sure healthier habits come into play on this build we call life.

Best Regards, Site Inspector

XIX

To The Elusive Concept of Love,

It must be so difficult to be misunderstood every single minute of the day. Each time you come out, someone thinks you're trying to attack them or that you have an ulterior motive. People do their best to express you but sometimes get it wrong out of fear. They try their best to use you in a healthy way and yet they mess it up. No one really knows how to embody you. Love, you're so evasive, we have a difficult time getting to know you. You're everywhere and yet, sometimes it feels like nowhere.

Love, I am so sorry that people keep messing up your identity. Some see you as abuse. Some see you as a sacrifice. People don't understand who you truly are. Maybe we've forgotten that to love someone as much as we want to, we have to find a way to love ourselves. How can we love someone so deep when we struggle at loving ourselves?

We haven't learned how to love yet.

I guess we have to teach ourselves how to have self love because no one else knows us as well as we do. What does loving ourselves look like?

If I went down that rabbit hole, I'd imagine you'd say that loving ourselves looks like accepting all of the pieces of us without judgment. Showing compassion to the demons within us and learning from our mistakes instead of using them as weapons on ourselves.

That is an interesting thought. To show compassion to our demons. I am curious to know your thoughts on it, Love. Because you could say you're the space that allows people to be their authentic selves. I genuinely don't know! So many people have tried to define you! How do you define yourself so we don't misunderstand you?

Best Regards, A Curious Human

XX

To The Daughter Who Grew Up with a Narcissistic Mother,

Labels limit.

They limit the person they seek to define. They limit your ability to see the person's potential. Narcissistic is another word for an unhealed trauma survivor.

So swish that around in your brain for a minute because the next part will be more difficult to read.

I'm sorry that your mother's parents didn't give her the tools to be a healthy mom. I'm sorry that she was abused. I'm sorry that you had to feel the product of that abuse. But you know what? She did her damndest to stop the cycle.

What you couldn't see behind closed doors was a mom racking her brain to figure out how to make her child's life healthier than her own childhood.

She knew that if she repeated the cycle she would create someone like herself. Someone who struggled through life without the tools.

Her being 'narcissistic' was the only angle you saw because she was tired of being put on the back burner. But she didn't know what else to do because it was the opposite of what her parents did. They put her on the back burner. So she thought putting herself on the front burner would be healthier. Not knowing it would raise children to have different struggles. So she did her best to remind her kids about how she took care of them. Not out of malice but out of, "Hey! Do you even recognize what I've done?" But kids can't. Not yet.

Healing isn't easy, and back then they didn't know what we know about healthy habits. She literally didn't have the resources to learn to heal herself.

So before you call your mom a narcissist, she was doing the best she could with the tools she had. Motherhood is something you never understand until you become a mother. You will always have a choice when you get older to decide how much time you spend with her.

Love, A Daughter Who Formerly Mislabeled Her Mother

XXI

To My Authentic Self,

I didn't realize. I didn't realize that I buried you so deep in my trauma that I became something I didn't recognize.

I never took time to stop the dirt from piling up. I just watched numbly, not knowing what would help or what would make it worse. So I did nothing.

The damage kept piling.

I'm sorry. I'm sorry that you're so deep in dirt that I can't even find you yet. I didn't have the tools to dig, but I'm ready now.

I'm ready to take my own shovel and start digging to uncover you, my authentic self. My identity doesn't rely on my trauma. I get to choose how I show up. How people perceive me is their perception. They will never see the bigger picture because they aren't me. I'm the only one who can see what needs to get done and how much worth I have.

And... that is okay. It's okay they don't see my worth.

I do.

So, I choose to dig.

No one else is going to do it for me. I have to take one shovel of dirt at a time.

It may be a long process, but I'm excited to find what I discover under all of that trauma. I am made of gold. I know to keep digging until I find my authentic golden self. Once I see my beauty and worth, people can't help but see it too. I have worth because I am human. Doesn't matter how many piles of dirt there are on top. I am worth digging up all of my shit to get to the gold.

With Love, Your Human

XXII

To My Soul,

You've communicated to me an interesting thought.

You said:

> *"Isn't it beautiful that you are human and spirit. Spirit can't say this."*

Soul, it has haunted me ever since you told me. Every human experience is something spirit cannot feel. Spirit can't smell the roses. Can't kiss a lover. Can't feel pain. Can't feel joy.

To be forever an outsider looking in at a tiny scene like watching a snow globe. Unable to touch a human's existence and yet here it stays. It stays with me through the ups and downs calling me to see out of love. Not annoyance, not out of hurt, not out of anything other than love.

Spirit is quiet sometimes but maybe that means I'm seeing out of love or I'm not ready to listen. Sometimes my ego is louder and my spirit watches it with compassion. Spirit may not be a human but I know it's made out of pure love.

That phrase you used about spirit not being human has triggered something in me. A stream of gratitude for this life. Most people say "Oh, be grateful. There are people out there that have less than you." They are ignoring major players. Spirit and *you*. My soul. This can also apply to you.

You are with me like a passenger on a train but you cannot leave. You can't experience the outside world so you beg me to be grateful for the world I get to live in.

I'm sorry I wasn't listening before. Even though this life can be difficult, at least I can experience it. You and spirit can only watch me behind glass with smiles on your faces. Celebrating everything.

Thank you. Thank you for the reminder, soul, that I am human and spirit.

From here on out I will work on remembering that I am a hybrid. Human and spirit. To be grateful for this human experience. Neither you nor spirit can say that. Again, I am grateful to be both human and spirit.

Love, Your Human

XXIII

To The Glass Ceiling,

I built you inside my mind. I thought I was worthless so I capped my potential at what I thought was my best. In reality, I have no idea of my potential because anything is possible.

Anything is possible because energy is the stem cell of the universe and we are all made out of energy. Literally anything is possible.

Glass ceiling, I don't think I need you anymore. You're there because I put you there during a time I did not know my worth. I know my worth now. Which means I can replace you with a glass window that opens. I don't need you to limit my potential anymore.

So many people already try to do that for me. Why am I being one of those people that limits me?

You were there for a season when I thought I needed you. I see my worth now. I no longer want to limit myself with a self-built glass ceiling.

With Respect, Your Human

XXIV

To The Piece of Happiness Inside,

I have a secret for you.

You don't have to jump off that cliff. You don't have to abandon all hope.

I know that life seems scary right now and hearing other people say that we need to worry doesn't help.

What if you changed "worry" to "prepare"? That's it. Just a friendly reminder that doom and gloom isn't imminent if you prepare. Basically, don't do shit that will make you worry. If you're afraid of the future, educate yourself on that topic and truly understand it. Then you'll know how to handle it.

If you can trust yourself to handle it, there's no point worrying about the future.

I've already taught you, little piece of happiness, to make an appearance every day. I taught you how to shine by proving that happiness is a mindset, not an emotion. You can definitely be felt, but that's the outward manifestation of what goes on in the brain. If you can practice how to show up every day then I wouldn't have to keep talking you down off a ledge. It's safe to make an appearance every day. You're allowed to shine. You're my piece of happiness.

Everyone is allowed to see you shine.

I'm tired of you peeking around corners and trying to jump off cliffs. It's okay to be you. Thank you for being a piece of me. I enjoy being happy. You don't have to be shy or afraid to show up during the day.

With Love, Your Human

XXV

To The One Who Chose To Stay,

Thank you.

I know I have a lot of history. I know my communication skills are a work in progress. I know I am working daily at healing. I know I am not perfect.

Regardless of that, you stay. You see me for who I am, not just the damage from my past. You meet me where I'm at each day. You see my quirky side and choose to love it.

You didn't have to stay, but you did. You have loved me at my best and my worst. Your patience is beyond my comprehension. I am grateful for you.

I see the burdens you carry on a daily basis and yet you choose to remain kind. Your life is alchemic. You didn't let the pain change you for the worst. You somehow transformed it to gold.

That's what alchemy is. Taking a crappy piece of rock and turning it into gold. You took a shitty situation and you stayed kind. Which allowed you to have the capability of unconditional love. Thank you.

I can only imagine how much strength it took to fight every day to take responsibility for your own happiness and share it with the world. I am just one of many that you have influenced. I know I keep saying this, but I am beyond grateful for your example of what unconditional love looks like.

You've allowed me to be completely me even if you may have disagreed with my decisions. I never once felt like you weren't on my side. You have always respected my emotions and let me process them at my own pace. For that, I am eternally grateful.

I think the key to your success is that you hold the belief that "change is the only constant" from the philosopher Heraclitus. You knew not to fall in love with the season I was in but to embrace the journey. I look back and I am grateful that you stayed. You have taught me a lot just by being you. You set a good example for me. Thank you for staying.

With Love, Someone Who Has Had People Leave

XXVI

Dear Time,

I have to say, you're weird. Some may say you're like smoke in the wind but I have a different theory.

The way I see it you're like a wave on the beach. You're here one moment and then gone the next.

I know it's coming as waves do. You're always marching as they say. But when waves break against sand or cliff it's a snapshot of grandeur. Either it's peaceful or it's explosive. Water smoothly glides across the sand as it returns to the sea or it splashes everything as it's pulled by gravity down against the rocks. Granted, I am not a surfer so I am sure there are more than two types of waves.

Time, you're exactly like a wave. Moments come and go. Sometimes you leave evidence that you were there, like a shell or even a shark tooth! Sometimes it's a carcass of a sea animal and it's heavy and needs to be dealt with or it starts to rot.

It really depends on what we pick up from that moment.

Waves are never the same. Just like moments of you. Time, the best way to experience you is to keep walking along the beach. Every wave that hits my toes or splashes my face I will embrace. I may not like some waves because they may try to pull me under but I choose to go back on dry land to get my bearings.

Same with life.

When I feel like a moment is dragging me under, I take a step back and take a break. I don't avoid it, but I do my best to observe from a distance, learning from the bigger picture. The ocean is the same way. Spend enough time at the beach and you get familiar with the tides. The ebb and flow of the water. The creatures, the locals. It becomes more comfortable to be in an ever-evolving environment. The ocean is never still. Neither is life. Time, thank you for being weird. You keep life interesting. Thank you for the 24 hours I have each day. I will choose what I pick up along the way on the beach of life.

With Love, Someone Who Almost Got Pulled Under

XXVII

To My Invisible Mirror,

I call you invisible because sometimes you're so close I can't see that you're there. I don't see that you're a mirror.

It's painful. I'm blinded by rage that I don't realize I'm not mad at you... I'm mad at myself.

I didn't realize that what you're doing bothers me because you're doing things that I do. I attracted you. My energy attracts who I am. I have to change myself to attract something different.

If I want you to change, I have to change myself first. Not for you. Not for anyone else. Nothing like that. I genuinely don't want to change you. I want to change to have peace.

You see, when I finally notice you, it all makes sense. I do what you do. You will always frustrate me until I change the person I see in the mirror.

I can't keep blaming the image I see in the mirror for something I created within myself. It's not easy and I'm exhausted from all the change, but the more I evolve, the more peace I have. I will never be perfect but that's okay.

I'm sorry I tried to hurt you, invisible mirror. I didn't realize what I was doing. I'm in pain. I've had a lot of fucked up shit happen and I am flying blind.

I admit I have trust issues. I've had my fair share of people leaving. No one's fault. People grow. They leave. They die. You name it. They embody the statement "change is the only constant" from Heraclitus.

I can't be upset at something I know is real. Change is real. Growth is real. Sometimes growing pains aren't physical but mental.

Invisible mirror, I understand why you had to stay invisible for so long. I wasn't ready to admit that you were there. It's not always easy looking in the mirror.

I don't always recognize myself because sometimes it's ugly.

I'll do better with taking care of you. You teach me a lot and I am grateful. I'll work on recognizing that you're there so I don't take my anger out on you and shatter you into a million pieces. It just multiplies the reflections of me and creates more pain.

I want to look at myself and want to heal so I don't spread my pain. Thank you for being visible now. You can be anyone that reflects what I need to change. It's scary but it helps. Thank you.

With Love, Your Human

XXVIII

To The One Who Is Too Much to Handle,

I can imagine it's lonely...

To be authentic means you have to be okay with who accepts you and who doesn't.

You're just being you and doing the best you can, and yet it doesn't feel like enough. You've been through so much that you feel like you don't have the energy or strength to keep trying with people. So people leave because you're living your life how you want to. You're not going with the flow of society and sometimes that creates choppy seas.

It's exhausting being authentic with loud energy. You're seen in a light that isn't always the best and yet you know that's their perception of you. You're just trying to be you.

It hurts. I know. It hurts to feel so alone. Feel like you don't fit in. Maybe none of us do. Maybe if we were all our authentic selves there wouldn't be division. Just unique people enjoying each other's company.

It takes strength to do what you're doing. I see it. Your eyes are heavy with the strength it takes to be you in a society that demands conformity.

I wish I could give you a hug and say, "it's better to be you, than keep up a lie." I wish I could give you the time and space you need to slow down and get to know yourself and what you need to replenish. I wish for a lot of things but just know you're doing it. You're doing what others dream about.

So as your head hits the pillow, smile, because you're you and no one else. Even if it takes work.

With Love, Your Human

XXIX

To The Abandoned One,

I know it wasn't your choice. You didn't ask to be abandoned. It feels empty, lonely, confusing, maddening, hurtful and every emotion in between.

I wanted to write to you and say, it wasn't because of you. Yes, it takes two to tango as the saying goes, but their choice was exactly that. Their choice.

You are not in charge of their choices, emotions, or consequences for their actions. To be abandoned feels so much like rejection, it's confusing. You're stuck with some of the pieces of the puzzle but no picture on the box to put the puzzle back together. So you do your best and you make a wonky picture out of the pieces.

My question to you is, why are you still using the pieces they left? You have a choice to build the puzzle they left behind or get a totally new box. Yes, it is a metaphor. They chose to leave. Not because you did anything wrong per se but rather you forced them to see pieces of themselves they didn't like.

That isn't easy. They didn't know what was happening. They didn't realize what they saw in you were lessons they needed to learn and vice versa. There were lessons you needed as well. They just chose to avoid the lessons. Mind you, those lessons might have been needed but maybe not at that moment.

They may have left because they didn't know how to love themselves. The way people treat you is exactly how they treat themselves. If they chose to leave, most likely than not they don't show up for themselves or they need space in order to figure themselves out first. There are so many reasons why someone leaves.

You have no control over that. What you have control over is your actions. Your thoughts. Your emotions and how you respond to their choice of leaving. Let them go…

Seriously, let them go. They aren't here any more. They chose not to be here so why are you so focused on keeping them here when they don't even want to enjoy this life with you? It's their loss. Obviously that does not mean forget them. But don't allow their choice of leaving, get you stuck in a moment.

Learn from them. Staying isn't always a pleasant thing when they haven't learned to love themselves yet. Only when you've learned to love and accept all that you are and that person has too, will it work out. Doesn't matter what title they hold in your life, it's still true. You don't have to be cold towards them but try to understand them and have grace because you're no better than them. You're learning lessons triggered by them leaving and they are learning lessons from leaving.

You got this.

With Love, Someone Who Chooses On A Daily Basis To Not let Someone's Choice Negatively Affect The Present

XXX

To My Anxiety,

I appreciate you. No, really, I do.

Here's why. You're trying to protect me by giving me more adrenaline to run. More escape plans. More ideas to keep myself safe by running various scenarios in my head to prepare for.

I'm grateful for you because it's like a little message to remind me I can use that energy towards something better. I could be sending good thoughts towards others. How can I be anxious if I'm too focused on wishing people good luck?

Anxiety, I'm grateful for you, but I trust myself to handle anything that comes my way. You don't have to worry for me. I got this.

Love, Your Human

XXXI

To My Inner Strength,

I read somewhere that strength is the ability to give yourself hope. While it sounds simple, it's a lot to accomplish.

I can imagine that it takes a lot to be able to say, "It's okay. This can't last forever. Better days are coming" and believe it. Especially when everything seems bleak.

Inner strength, you're something I am grateful for. I didn't realize I had it until people told me "you are strong".

It took a while for me to believe them. In the moment it didn't help hearing it. If anything, it would frustrate me because that's not how I felt.

In the moment that you were shining inner strength, my world felt pitch black. I didn't feel strong when I gave myself hope. I felt the opposite.

But as I look back and see the progress in my life because of my inner strength, I see how valuable you are. Inner strength, you shine when it's the darkest.

If it's light all the time there's no need for inner strength because there is no need for strength. Everything is good in the light.

We need dark moments to balance out the light. Both have lessons for us. I am grateful for you, my inner strength.

With Love, Your Human

XXXII

To The Unhealed Version of Me,

Thank you.

Two words that hold so much weight when it's said by the right person.

I hope you can feel the depth of gratitude I have for you. You've been in the trenches.

You have survived a lot and for that I am grateful. Because, without you, there is no me.

We did it! We figured it out! Maybe not all of it, and that's okay. But I have way more neutral responses and I've become aware of my ego more. I do my best to speak out of love. Sometimes I fuck up.

But I always do my best to learn from my "mistakes." I look at them now as lessons instead of inflictors of pain. I didn't realize I was standing there holding the whip.

I found out from Eckhart Tolle that the past can only hurt us if we let it. It happened in the past. Apparently, if I focus too much on the future I get anxious. So it's like a tightrope walker. Doing my best to live in the moment. Sometimes there are wobbles and I go back and forth from the past to worrying about the future, but the more I practice, the steadier the line and less wobbles.

I haven't enjoyed life this much in a very long time. I haven't been this confident in my entire life. To have compassion for myself and live in the moment. It's okay to be happy and learn how to heal!!! You've been through a lot. Don't let anyone shit on your parade. Seriously!! Don't!!

Unhealed version of me, I'm grateful for you. You're the one that got me here. Thank you for being a part of my life.

Love, The Ever-Evolving Human

XXXIII

To The Unseen,

You've come to the end.

I hope you feel a little better after reading this book.

I feel like we've all forgotten how to be genuine... we've forgotten to have compassion...

We're all on the same level. We all suffer. That's the whole message with the arrangement of this book. We all suffer, but it's up to us for how long.

As I mentioned, I didn't originally write these letters for an audience. I wrote them to myself, and now I've arranged the letters to tell a story of growth for an audience.

This book is something very special to me because I am being truly genuine. I am being my authentic self, and I don't care who doesn't accept it. The book was created because the letters hold weight and empowerment and

I hope these letters have made some sort of impact on you. Good or bad. Doesn't matter. I want you to experience this life exactly how you want to.

You are in charge of your own life. Your thoughts turn into actions. If you can change your thoughts, you can change how you experience this life. That is what I learned from the ages of 28 to 31.

If you're asking yourself what happened during those years, it doesn't matter. The real question is: Do you feel less alone in the world?

Until next time.

Love, Rosie

References

Dispenza, D. J. (2019). *Becoming Supernatural*. HAY HOUSE UK LTD.

Hall, N. (2021, May 25). *Newton's Laws of Motion - Glenn Research Center*. NASA. Retrieved November 10, 2021, from https://www1.grc.nasa.gov/beginners-guide-to-aeronautics/newtons-laws-of-motion/.

Hanh, T. N. (1998). *The Heart of the Buddha's Teaching*. Harmony Books.

Harari, Y. N. (2022). *Sapiens: A Brief History of Humankind*. Signal.

Heraclitus, Patrick, G. T. W., & Bywater, I. (1889). *The Fragments of the Work of Heraclitus of Ephesus on Nature: Translated from the Greek text of Bywater, with an introd. historical and critical*. Baltimore: N. Murray.

J.M.K.C. Donev et al. (2021). Energy Education - Law of Conservation of Energy [Online]. Available: https://energyeducation.ca/encyclopedia/Law_of_conservation_of_energy. [Accessed: November 10, 2021].

Tolle, E. (2018). *The Power of Now: A Guide to Spiritual Enlightenment*. Hachette Australia.

Printed in Great Britain
by Amazon